Set 1

Dictionary Skills

- definitions
- guide words
- entry words
- pronunciation key
- parts of speech
- syllables
- accent marks

Answer Form
Set 1

Name _____

1. _____

   _____

   _____

2. _____

3. _____

   _____

4. _____

5.

6. _____

   _____

   _____

7. _____

   _____

8. _____

9. _____

10. _____

11. _____

12. _____

    _____

    _____

13. _____

    _____

14. _____

15. _____

    _____

16. _____

    _____

17. _____

    _____

18. _____

19. _____

    _____

20. _____

21. _____

22. _____

23. _____

    _____

24. _____

    _____

25. _____

    _____

26. _____

    _____

27. _____

28. _____

29. _____

30. _____

    _____

31. _____

    _____

32. _____

Answer Key
Set 1

1. Answers will vary.
2. (c) silhouette
3. 43,560 square feet
4. yellow
5.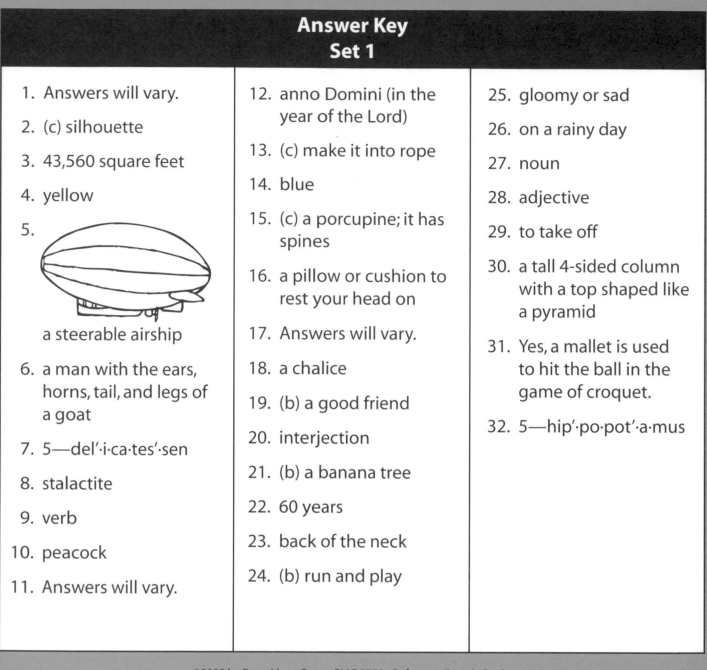
   a steerable airship
6. a man with the ears, horns, tail, and legs of a goat
7. 5—del'·i·ca·tes'·sen
8. stalactite
9. verb
10. peacock
11. Answers will vary.

12. anno Domini (in the year of the Lord)
13. (c) make it into rope
14. blue
15. (c) a porcupine; it has spines
16. a pillow or cushion to rest your head on
17. Answers will vary.
18. a chalice
19. (b) a good friend
20. interjection
21. (b) a banana tree
22. 60 years
23. back of the neck
24. (b) run and play

25. gloomy or sad
26. on a rainy day
27. noun
28. adjective
29. to take off
30. a tall 4-sided column with a top shaped like a pyramid
31. Yes, a mallet is used to hit the ball in the game of croquet.
32. 5—hip'·po·pot'·a·mus

©2005 by Evan-Moor Corp. • EMC 2750 • Reference Search Cards

- - - - - - - - - - - fold - - - - - - - - - - -

2

Which of these is the correct spelling for "an outline portrait cut out of black paper"?

   a. siloette

   b. sillouette

   c. silhouette

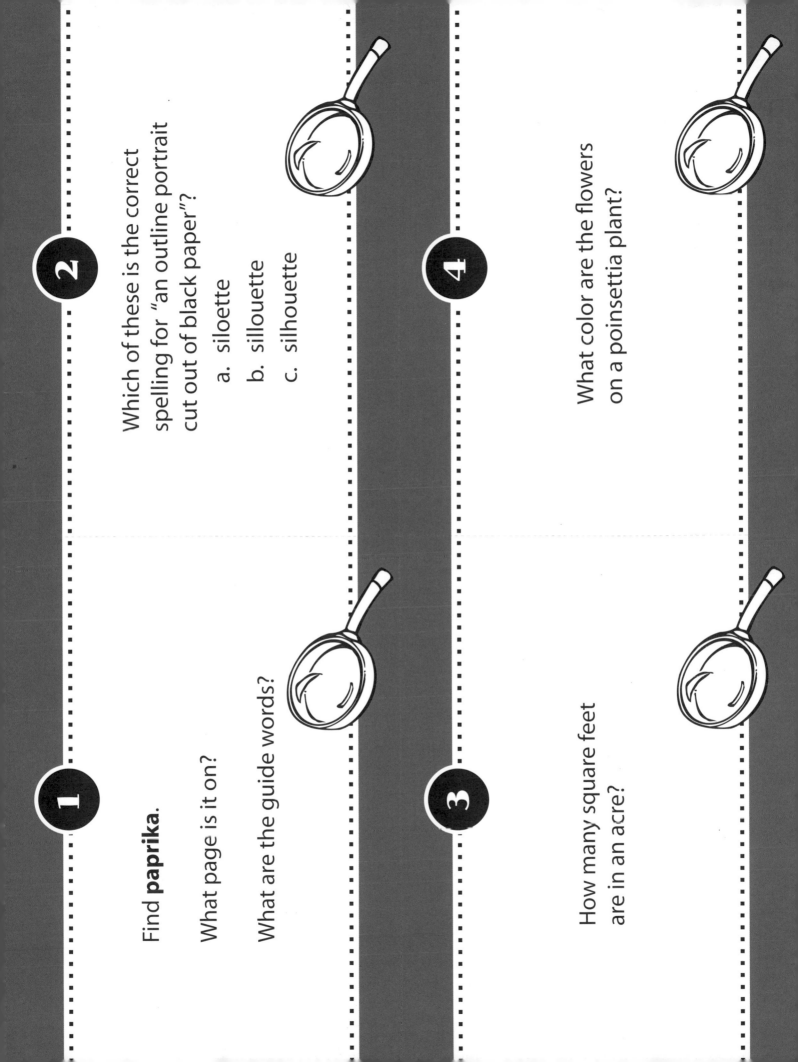

4

What color are the flowers on a poinsettia plant?

1

Find **paprika**.

What page is it on?

What are the guide words?

3

How many square feet are in an acre?

Set 1

Set 1

Set 1

Set 1

6

What would a **faun** look like?

8

Which one hangs from the ceiling, a **stalagmite** or a **stalactite**?

5

Draw or describe a **dirigible**.

7

How many syllables are in **delicatessen**?

Where do the accent marks go?

Set 1

Set 1

Set 1

Set 1

10

How do you spell **pe'·kok**?

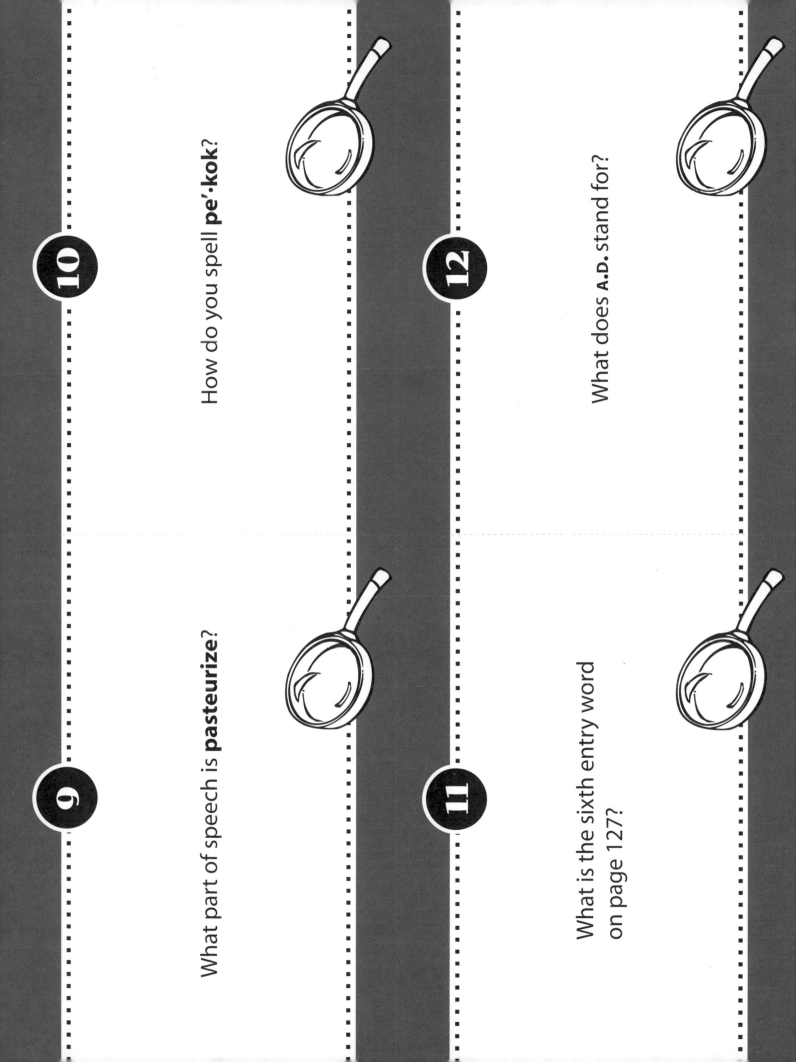

12

What does A.D. stand for?

9

What part of speech is **pasteurize**?

11

What is the sixth entry word on page 127?

Set 1

Set 1

Set 1

Set 1

14

What color is **indigo**?

13

How would you use **jute**?

a. play a tune on it
b. cook it for dinner
c. make it into rope

16

What is a **bolster** used for?

15

A **hedgehog** is more like _____.

a. a peccary
b. an anteater
c. a porcupine

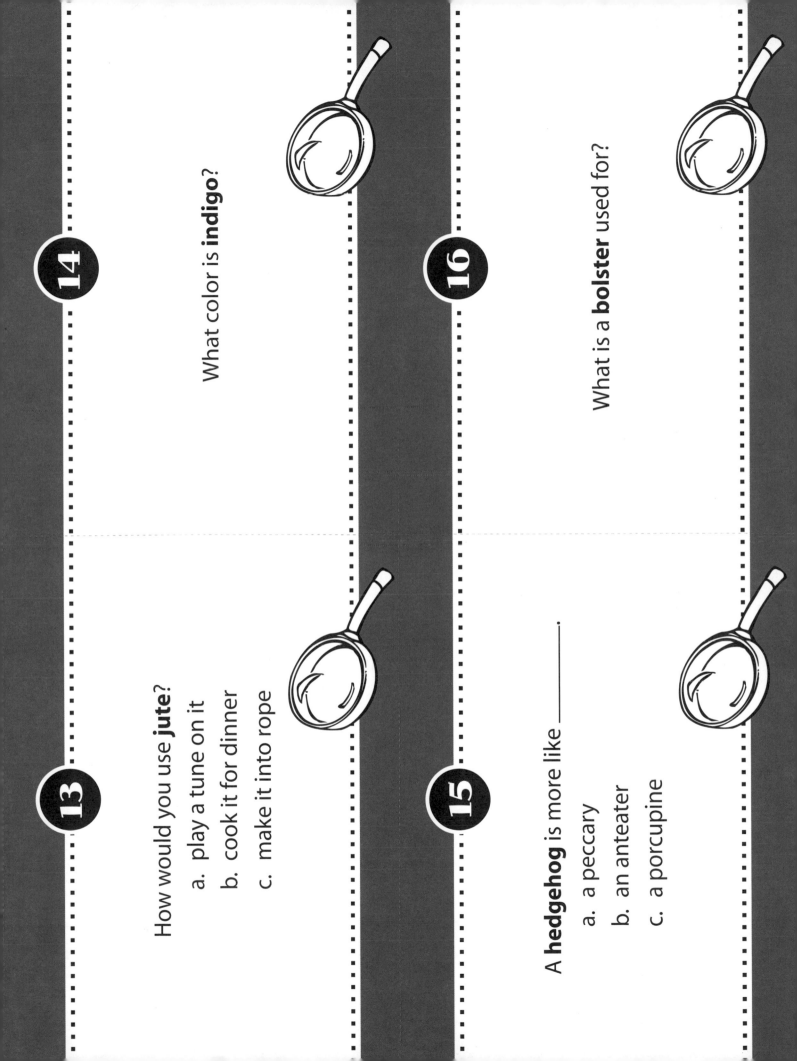

Set 1

Set 1

Set 1

Set 1

18

Would you drink from
a **chalice** or an **urn**?

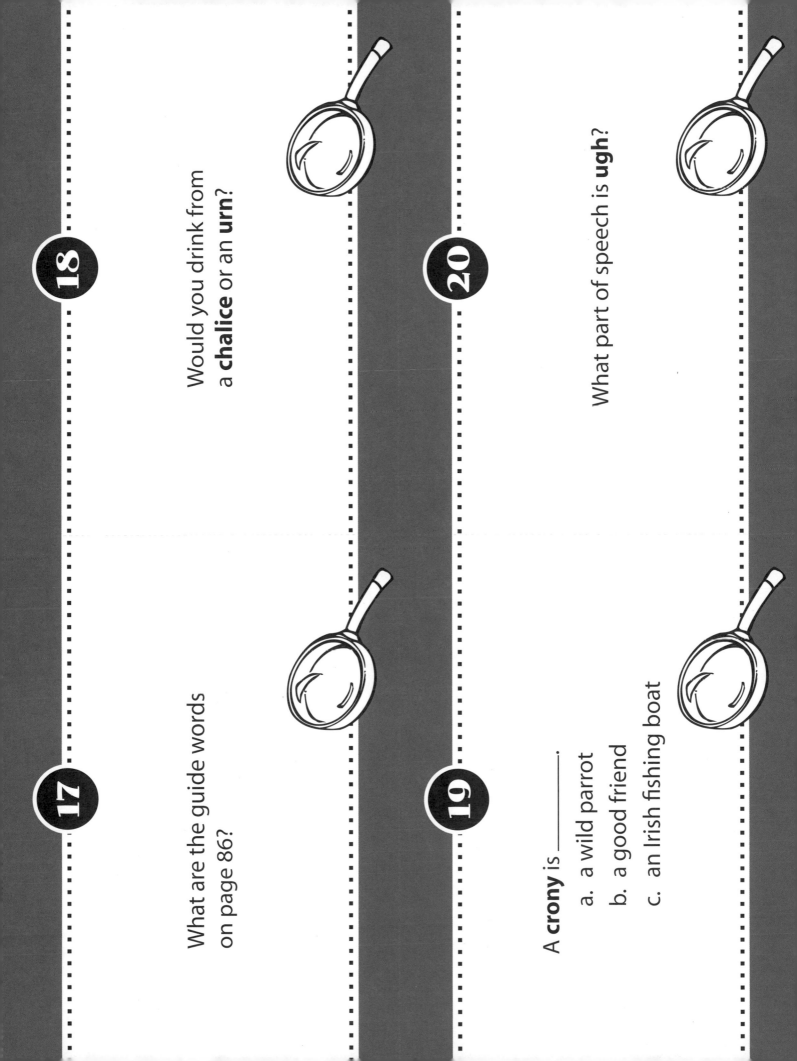

20

What part of speech is **ugh**?

17

What are the guide words
on page 86?

19

A **crony** is _____.

a. a wild parrot

b. a good friend

c. an Irish fishing boat

Set 1

Set 1

Set 1

Set 1

22

How long is **threescore** years?

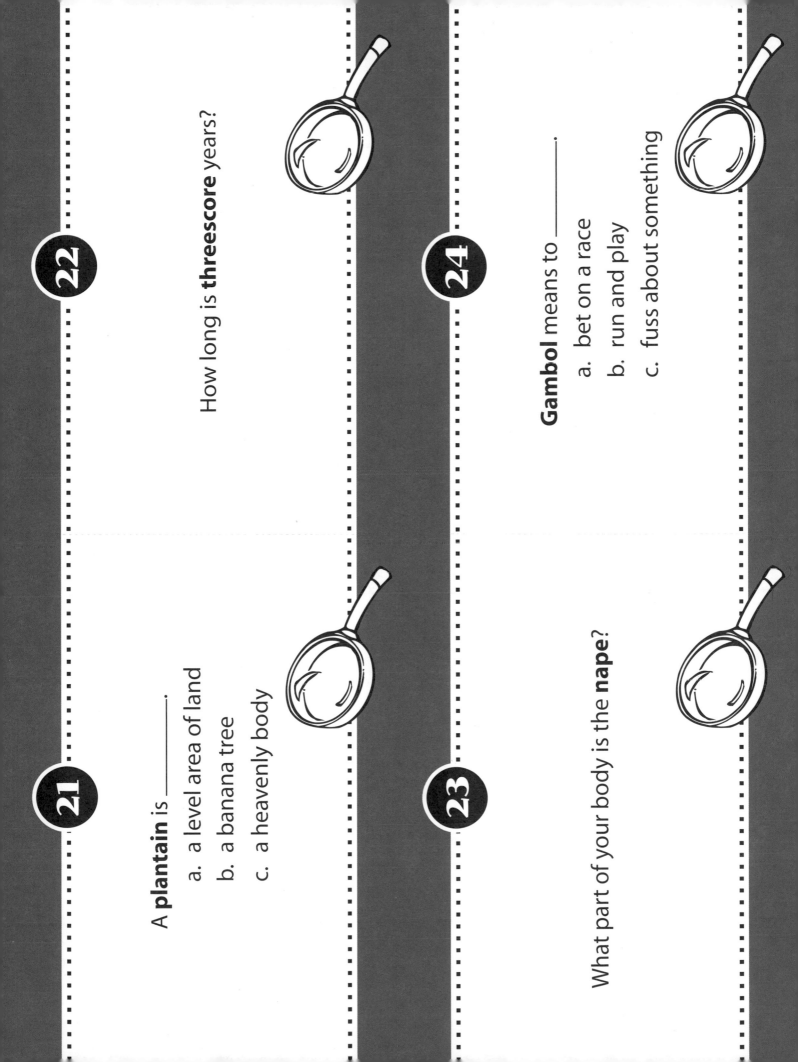

24

Gambol means to _____.

  a. bet on a race

  b. run and play

  c. fuss about something

21

A **plantain** is _____.

  a. a level area of land

  b. a banana tree

  c. a heavenly body

23

What part of your body is the **nape**?

Set 1

Set 1

Set 1

Set 1

26

When would you wear **galoshes**?

28

What part of speech is **thunderstruck**?

25

How does a **melancholy** person feel?

27

What part of speech is **urchin**?

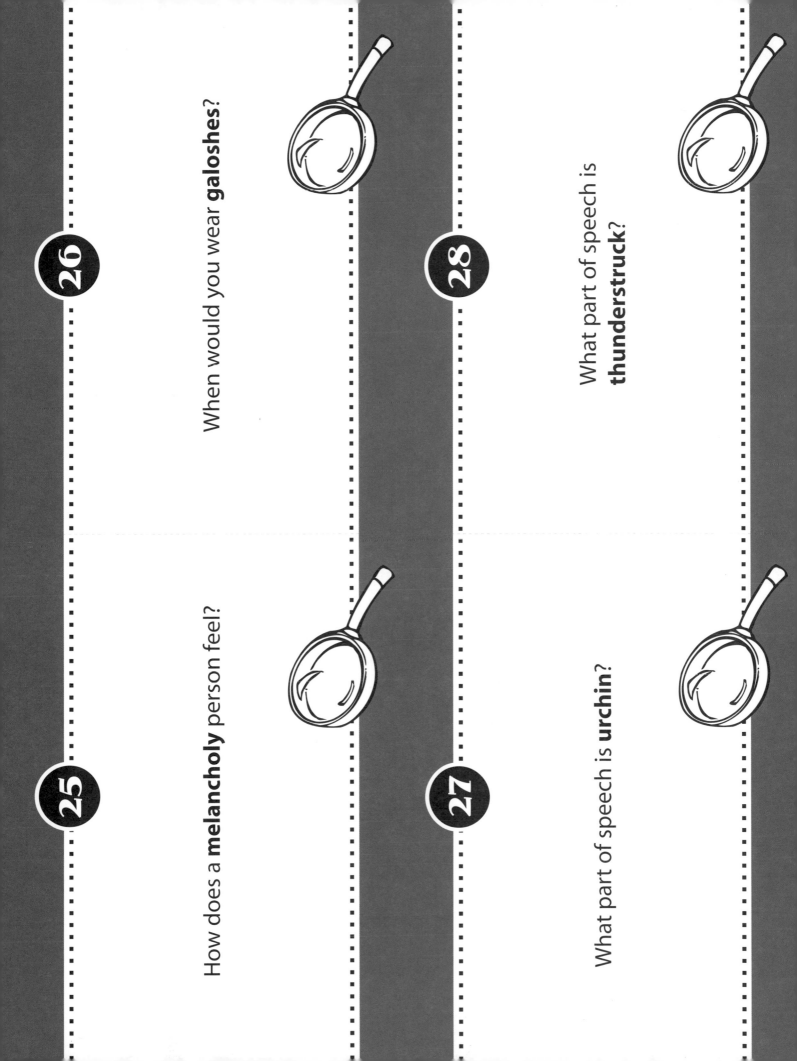

Set 1

Set 1

Set 1

Set 1

30

What shape is an **obelisk**?

32

How many syllables are in **hippopotamus?**

Where do the accent marks go?

29

Does **doff** mean "to put on" or "to take off"?

31

Would you use a **mallet** in **croquet?**

Why or why not?

Set 1

Set 1

Set 1

Set 1

Encyclopedia Skills

- alphabetical order
- locate information
- scan articles
- guide words
- index
- maps
- charts
- diagrams

Answer Form

Set 2

Name _____

1. _____

2. _____

3. _____

_____

_____

4. _____

5. _____

_____

6. _____

7. _____

_____

8. _____

_____

9. _____

10. _____

11. _____

12. _____

13. _____

_____

_____

14. _____

15. _____

_____

16. _____

_____

17. _____

_____

18. _____

_____

19. _____

_____

20. _____

_____

21. _____

_____

22. _____

23. _____

24. _____

_____

25. _____

26. _____

27. _____

_____

_____

28. _____

29. _____

30. _____

_____

_____

31. a. _____

b. _____

c. _____

32. _____

_____

fold

1. Edwin E. Aldrin, Jr.
2. Fort Sumter, South Carolina
3. 12 letters (a e i o u h k l m n p w)
4. Greenland
5. James A. Naismith
6. Cullinan
7. saurischians and ornithischians
8. whale shark; 60 feet
9. 14
10. (c) Andrew Jackson
11. 33
12. John Adams, John Quincy Adams, John F. Kennedy, or George H. W. Bush
13. Manhattan, the Bronx, Queens, Brooklyn, and Staten Island
14. Poseidon
15. the Mariana Trench
16. clay and graphite
17. Westmoreland County, Virginia (Bridges Creek Plantation, Wakefield)
18. Central and South America (tropical areas)
19. the second-highest mountain in the world (sometimes called Mount Godwin Austen)
20. incisor, canine (cuspid), premolar (bicuspid), and molar
21. Wilhelm Roentgen; 1895
22. Central Africa
23. an aerie
24. malleus (hammer), incus (anvil), and stapes (stirrup)
25. Mozart
26. 1781
27. the rights to freedom of worship, speech, press, and assembly
28. a portrait painter
29. younger
30. at the top; the last entry on the page
31. Answers will vary.
32. topics in alphabetical order and the volume and page number(s) where each topic is found

©2005 by Evan-Moor Corp. • EMC 2750 • Reference Search Cards

- fold -

2

Where was the first battle of the Civil War fought?

4

Where do North Atlantic icebergs come from?

1

Who accompanied Neil Armstrong on the first lunar landing?

3

How many letters are in the Hawaiian alphabet?

What are they?

Set 2

Set 2

Set 2

Set 2

6

What is the name of the largest diamond discovered so far?

8

What is the largest fish?

How long does it grow?

5

Who invented the game of basketball?

7

What are the names of the two major groups of dinosaurs?

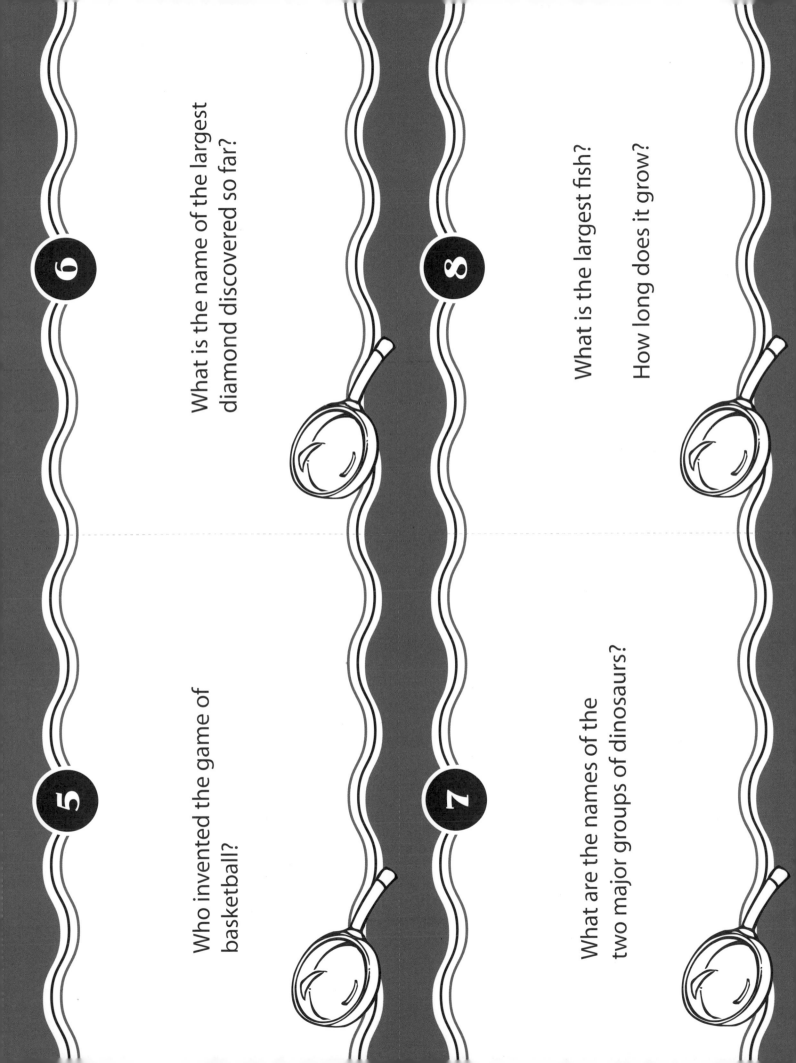

Set 2

Set 2

Set 2

Set 2

10

Which one was the seventh president of the United States?

   a. James Monroe

   b. John Tyler

   c. Andrew Jackson

12

Name one of the presidents who came from Massachusetts.

9

What is the maximum number of golf clubs that can be used during a regulation round of golf?

11

How old was Thomas Jefferson when he wrote the Declaration of Independence?

Set 2

Set 2

Set 2

Set 2

14

What was the Greek name for the god Neptune?

16

What is the lead in a pencil made of?

13

Name the five boroughs of New York City.

15

What is the deepest part of the ocean?

Set 2

Set 2

Set 2

Set 2

18

Where are vampire bats found?

20

Name the four types of human teeth.

17

Where was George Washington born?

19

What is K-2?

Set 2

Set 2

Set 2

Set 2

22

Where is Zaire located?

24

Name the three smallest bones
in your ear.

21

Who discovered the X-ray?

In what year?

23

What is an eagle's nest called?

Set 2

Set 2

Set 2

Set 2

26

In what year was the planet Uranus discovered?

28

What was Joshua Reynolds' occupation?

25

Who wrote *The Magic Flute*?

27

What is the first amendment to the United States Constitution?

Set 2

Set 2

Set 2

Set 2

30

Where are guide words shown on an encyclopedia page?

What does the guide word on the right-hand page stand for?

32

What kind of information is in the Guide or Index volume of the encyclopedia?

29

Was Orville Wright older or younger than his brother Wilbur?

31

On what page of Volume 1 of an encyclopedia can you find an example of each of these?

a. a chart

b. a map

c. a diagram

Set 2

Set 2

Set 2

Set 2

Atlas Skills

- locate information
- read physical maps
- read political maps
- longitude and latitude
- index

Answer Form

Set 3

Name _____

1. _____

2. _____

3. _____

4. _____

5. _____

6. _____

7. _____

8. _____

   _____

9. _____

   _____

10. _____

    _____

11. _____

12. _____

13. _____

_____

14. _____

15. _____

_____

16. _____

17. _____

18. _____

19. _____

_____

20. _____

21. _____

22. _____

_____

23. _____

24. _____

25. _____

26. _____

27. _____

28. _____

29. _____

30. _____

31. _____

32. a. _____

    b. _____

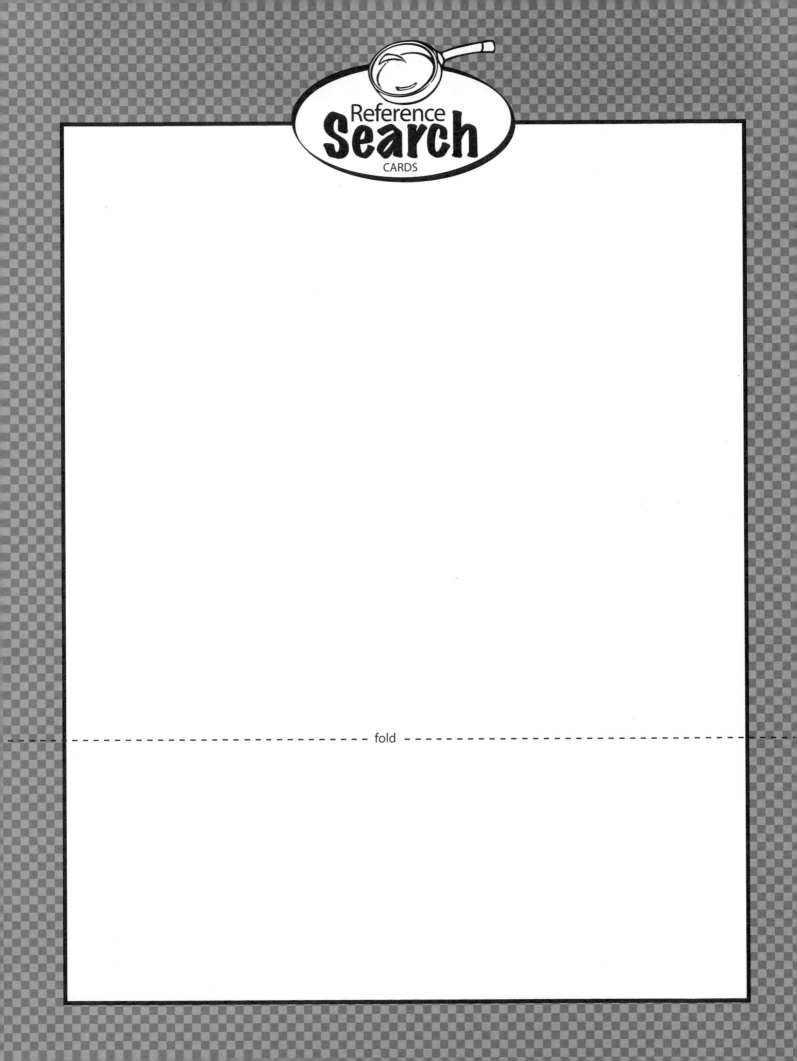

Reference
Search
CARDS

- - - - - - - - - - - - - - - fold - - - - - - - - - - - - - - -

Answer Key
Set 3

1. Alaska
2. Brazil
3. Indian Ocean
4. Antarctica
5. Nairobi
6. Oahu
7. Seine
8. north; west
9. Gulf of St. Lawrence
10. New Orleans, Louisiana
11. 5:00
12. Queensland
13. Mediterranean Sea
14. Caribbean Sea
15. Colorado, Oklahoma, Missouri, and Nebraska
16. Russia
17. Pyrenees
18. the equator
19. Sweden, Finland, Russia
20. Australia
21. Georgia
22. England and France
23. Gulf of Mexico
24. Madagascar
25. Bering Strait
26. south
27. Arizona
28. compass rose
29. Arctic Ocean
30. the prime meridian
31. Nicaragua
32. (a) longitude; (b) latitude

©2005 by Evan-Moor Corp. • EMC 2750 • Reference Search Cards

- - - - - - - - - - - - - - - - - - fold - - - - - - - - - - - - - - - - - -

Set 3

Which South America country has the largest land area?

2

On which continent will you find the South Pole?

4

Where is Denali National Park located?

1

What ocean lies between Africa and Australia?

3

Set 3

Set 3

Set 3

Set 3

Reference Search

On which of the Hawaiian Islands is the capital city located?

6

Reference Search

What is the capital of Kenya?

5

Reference Search

Is Jamaica north or south of the equator?

Is it east or west of the prime meridian?

8

Reference Search

What river flows between Paris and the English Channel?

7

Set 3

Set 3

Set 3

Set 3

Reference Search

9

In what gulf will you find Prince Edward Island?

Reference Search

10

What city in the USA will you find at 30°N 90°W?

Reference Search

11

If it is 8:00 in New York City, what time is it in San Francisco, California?

Reference Search

12

The Great Barrier Reef is off the coast of which state in Australia?

Set 3

Set 3

Set 3

Set 3

Reference Search

What sea surrounds Cyprus?

13

Reference Search

What sea lies off the coast of Venezuela?

14

Reference Search

Which states border Kansas?

15

Reference Search

What country is north of Mongolia?

16

Set 3

Set 3

Set 3

Set 3

Reference Search

What mountain range will you cross traveling from France to Spain?

17

Reference Search

What is 0° latitude called?

18

Reference Search

What three countries border Norway?

19

Reference Search

On what continent will you find the Great Victoria Desert?

20

Set 3

Set 3

Set 3

Set 3

Reference Search

Which state will you pass through traveling from South Carolina to Florida?

21

Reference Search

What countries border the English Channel?

22

Reference Search

What large body of water does southern Alabama touch?

23

Reference Search

What large island nation lies in the Indian Ocean off the eastern coast of Africa?

24

Set 3

Set 3

Set 3

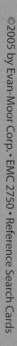

Set 3

Reference Search

What body of water would you cross traveling from Russia to Alaska?

25

Reference Search

Which direction is Tasmania from Australia?

26

Reference Search

In which state will you find the Grand Canyon?

27

Reference Search

Which part of a map helps you identify directions?

28

Set 3

Set 3

Set 3

Set 3

Reference Search

What is the special name
for 0° longitude?

30

Reference Search

Name each of these lines on a map:
a. lines going from north to south
b. lines going from east to west

32

Reference Search

What ocean is found
at the North Pole?

29

Reference Search

What country will you find
north of Costa Rica and
south of Honduras?

31

Set 3

Set 3

Set 3

Set 3

Almanac Skills

- alphabetical order
- locate information
- scan articles
- index
- charts
- tables
- graphs

Answer Form

Set 4

Reference Search CARDS

Name _____

1. _____

_____

2. _____

_____

3. _____

4. _____

_____

5. a. _____

   b. _____

6. _____

7. _____

_____

8. _____

9. a. _____

   b. _____

   c. _____

10. _____

11. _____

12. _____

13. _____

_____

14. _____

_____

15. _____

_____

16. _____

_____

17. _____

_____

18. _____

19. a. _____

    b. _____

    c. _____

20. _____

_____

21. _____

22. _____

_____

23. _____

24. a. _____

    b. _____

    c. _____

25. a. _____

    b. _____

    c. _____

26. _____

27. _____

_____

28. _____

29. _____

30. _____

31. _____

32. _____

Reference
Search
CARDS

- - - - - - - fold - - - - - - -

Answer Key
Set 4

1. cheetah—65 to 75 mph; snail—0.03 mph

2. Galápagos tortoise; 200+ years

3. French

4. the Boston Tea Party

5. (a) crescent moon and star;
   (b) dragon

6. Mercury

7. Yuri Gagarin; 1961

8. 12

9. (a) Canadian dollar;
   (b) yen;
   (c) won

10. hibiscus

11. Mandarin Chinese

12. (a) the Pentagon

13. President Ulysses S. Grant

14. Bolivia and Paraguay

15. John Adams, Thomas Jefferson, and James Monroe

16. green, yellow, red, black, and white

17. April 13, 1743; Shadwell, Virginia

18. kit, cub, or pup

19. (a) Dana Owens;
    (b) Chan Kwong-Sung;
    (c) Thomas Mapother IV

20. began in 1861; ended in 1865

21. A.D. 79

22. 1891; Whitcomb Judson

23. Hg

24. (a) eastern brown pelican;
    (b) cardinal;
    (c) bluebird

25. (a) Aphrodite;
    (b) Poseidon;
    (c) Zeus

26. the Nile

27. index; back of the book

28. Bering Sea

29. Sahara

30. Greenland

31. Ring of Fire

32. Answers will vary.

- - - - - - - - - - - - - - - - fold - - - - - - - - - - - - - - - - -

Set 4

2

What is the name of the longest-living animal?

How long does it live?

4

What happened in U.S. history on December 16, 1773?

1

How fast can a cheetah run?

How fast can a snail move?

3

What is the national language of the Democratic Republic of the Congo?

Set 4

Set 4

Set 4

Set 4

6

Which is the fastest moving planet?

8

How many European countries use the euro as their national currency?

5

What picture is on each of these countries' flags?

a. Algeria

b. Bhutan

7

Who was the first man to orbit the Earth?

In what year did his flight take place?

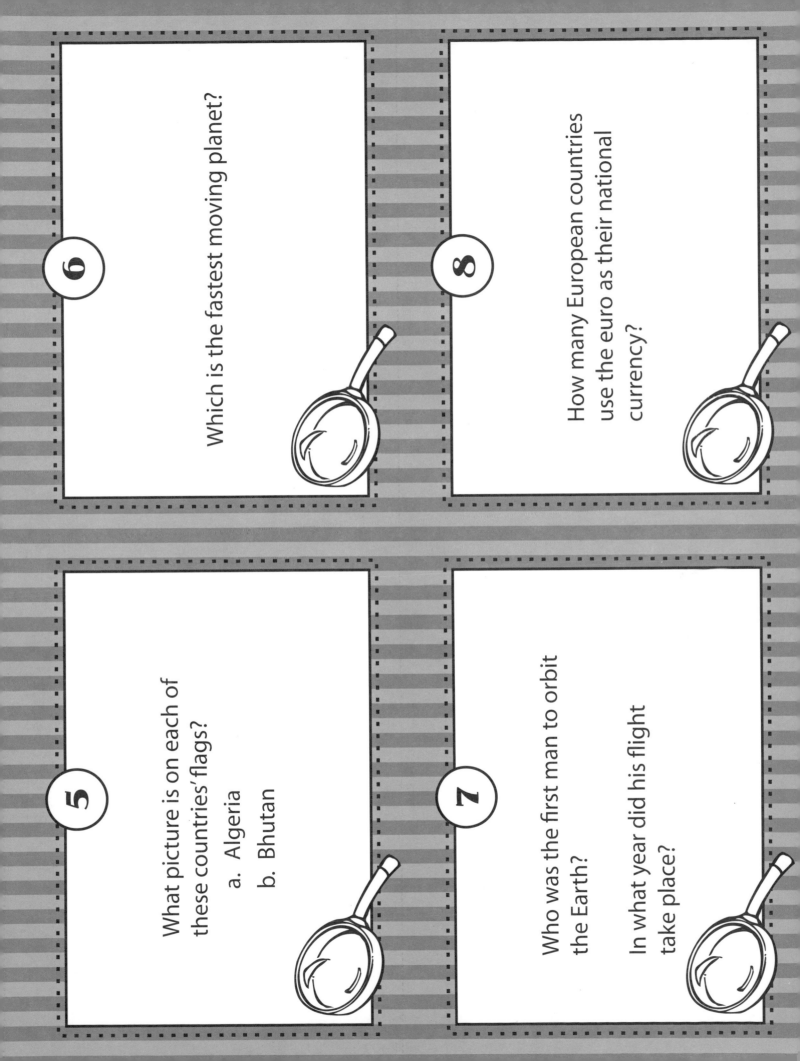

Set 4

Set 4

Set 4

Set 4

10

What is the state flower of Hawaii?

12

Which of these buildings is larger (in square feet)?

  a. the Pentagon, Washington, D.C.

  b. the Empire State Building, New York, NY

9

What currency is used by each of these countries?

  a. Canada

  b. Japan

  c. South Korea

11

What language is spoken by the most people in the world?

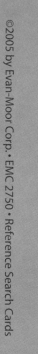

Set 4

Set 4

Set 4

Set 4

13

Who is pictured on the $50 bill?

14

Which two countries in South America are surrounded by land?

15

Which three United States presidents died on the fourth of July?

16

What colors are on the flag of Zimbabwe?

Set 4

Set 4

Set 4

Set 4

18

What is a young fox called?

20

When did the Civil War begin in the USA?

When did it end?

17

When and where was President Thomas Jefferson born?

19

What was the original name of each of the following?

a. Queen Latifah

b. Jackie Chan

c. Tom Cruise

Set 4

Set 4

Set 4

22

When was the zipper invented?

Who was the inventor?

24

What is the state bird of each of the following?
a. Louisiana
b. Illinois
c. Missouri

21

In what year did Mt. Vesuvius erupt in Italy, killing 16,000 people?

23

What is the chemical symbol for mercury?

Set 4

Set 4

Set 4

Set 4

26

Which river is longer, the Amazon or the Nile?

28

Into what sea does Alaska's Yukon River flow?

25

What is the Greek name for each of these Roman gods?

a. Venus

b. Neptune

c. Jupiter

27

What part of an almanac helps you quickly find the subject and the page it is on?

Where is it found in the almanac?

Set 4

Set 4

Set 4

Set 4

30

What is the biggest island on Earth?

32

On what page of the almanac does the "Sports" section begin?

29

What is the largest desert in the world?

31

What is the name of the area in which 75% of the world's volcanoes are located?

Set 4

Set 4

Set 4

Set 4